Letter to the Romans

A Small Group Bible Study Guide

PRESSED
THOUGHTS

LETTER TO THE ROMANS,
A SMALL GROUP
BIBLE STUDY GUIDE

Published by Pressed Thoughts LLC

www.pressedthoughts.com

ISBN 978-0-9850102-3-2

CONTENTS

DEDICATION

This book is dedicated to the good men of MCI-J, and incarcerated believers everywhere, that are brave enough to look honestly inside themselves; wise enough to overlook the failings of others; faithful enough to put their trust in God; humble enough to accept the free grace of His forgiveness; loving enough to share the gospel of Jesus Christ at times and places where it is difficult to do so; attentive enough to edify, encourage, and give hope in Christ to all their brothers and sisters in the faith; and shrewd enough to learn how to improve themselves so that they can do all these things more effectively.

.

THE SMALL GROUP BIBLE STUDY

The purpose of this guide is to support a small group Bible study of Paul's letter to the Romans. It is designed to encourage the participants to think deeper about what they are reading, to learn how to draw out wisdom that can be applied to their own lives, and also to see, through firsthand study, how the Bible, in its entirety, weaves together a tale of God's love for us.

An effective small group Bible study, however, has multiple goals. One, of course, is to facilitate the mutual, intellectual understanding of the text under study. Another, more important aspect of the group is to build closer relationships with one another. It makes no sense to mechanically lead a small group through a Bible study with steadfast determination. Sometimes it is important to take a break on this study of Christian love, so that the group can actually engage in Christian love. So as you move through the study, do not be afraid of tangential conversations and do not be afraid to even skip the scheduled study of the day if the Spirit is leading the group to spend a little time building intimacy or helping someone work through a life issue.

The chapters of this guide break the study of Romans into six lessons according to general topic; however, the questions within these chapters follow the book chronologically to enable the group to set their own pace of study. As a group, it is important to adjust the pace of the lessons based on the level of discussion activity

1

within each session.

Prior to studying Romans, it is worth reading through one or more of the Gospels as well as the book of Acts. If time permits the reading of only one of the Gospels, then the Gospel of Luke is a natural choice because Luke and Acts where penned by the same author. Paul's letter was intended to share and illuminate the gospel of Jesus, so reading Jesus' own words is a clear aid in understanding Paul. (The converse is also true, reading Paul's explanations can be an aid to understanding the Gospels.) The review of Acts is recommended because it provides significant historical context surrounding the time of the formation of the early churches and additionally provides a significant understanding of Paul as a person.

As you sit down to read the scriptures prior to each of these sessions, take the time to pray that the Holy Spirit guide you in your understanding of the text. And as you meet together as a group, pray for each other and pray that the Holy Spirit guide the discussion in a manner pleasing to the Lord.

HOW TO STUDY A BOOK OF THE BIBLE

A book of the Bible can be studied in many different ways and a student is free to go to whatever depth of study they desire. On the shelves of bookstores, you can find that authors have written whole volumes focusing on just a single verse of the scriptures.

The style of study this guide supports is a more cursory study that should leave the student with a fair understanding of the main messages of the book, thus leaving time for the student to continue with other areas of the Bible. Many have found that after they have read through and studied larger portions of the Bible at a higher level, their ability to understand each individual book is deepened.

To facilitate this study, begin by reading the entire letter to the Romans, cover to cover; then, as you proceed with the lessons, read through each set of chapters again with more care. It is often helpful to make notes on what you perceive as the key points of the text. You can then read the questions within this guide, making notes and writing down answers as you go.

It is strongly recommended that a Study Bible be used for this study and in an edition that is readable for you. If you are very comfortable reading old English, or just like a challenge, then the King James version may be for you. The majority of scripture passages used in this book are from the ESV Bible, which was translated with a philosophy of making the text readable, but to the extent possible, maintaining the form of the original Biblical texts.

Take the time to learn the cross reference system used by your particular study Bible and especially note that Study Bibles are meant to be *dirty* Bibles. As you read along, don't hesitate to underline meaningful verses, scribble notes in the margin, and otherwise markup your Bible.

Other Bible resources are available to aid in the study and should be used freely to help you gain further insight. Digital versions of the Bible are available online and also available for hand-held devices. These versions provide full-text word search capability that is ideal for locating and reading other passages of scripture that relate to the current study.

INTRODUCTION TO ROMANS

Eight years after Paul sent his letter to the churches in Rome in 58 AD, the apostle Peter, while in Rome, shared the following advice with fellow believers in regard to Paul's writing (2 Pet. 3:15-16): *And count the patience of our Lord as salvation, just as our beloved brother Paul also wrote to you according to the wisdom given him, as he does in all his letters when he speaks in them of these matters. There are some things in them that are hard to understand, which the ignorant and unstable twist to their own destruction, as they do the other Scriptures.*

It is clear from 1st Peter (64 AD) and 2nd Peter (66 AD), both of which Peter wrote while in Rome, that Peter was familiar with Paul's complex theological explanations and it is not hard to imagine that Peter, a fisherman by trade, had spent much time in Rome explaining them to the disciples within the city.

Much of what we know of Paul comes from Acts, Luke's historical account of the early church. Paul, known also by his Jewish name Saul, was a Jew born a Roman citizen in the city of Tarsus. There, he received a thorough education in the Greek language, culture, and history. He was then sent to attend rabbinical school in Jerusalem where he studied under the most prominent rabbi of the day, receiving a thorough education in the ancient scriptures. Paul was so devoted to Judaism that he became a Pharisee, a group of deeply religious people who believed that a strict adherence to the Laws of Moses led to salvation. As a brilliant scholar, Paul was able to view and reason the scriptures both from a Jewish historical point of view as well as from a Greek rational point of view. Three years after his conversion, Paul sought out Peter and the other apostles to visit them and during this visit he almost certainly learned much from them. It is unclear how much of the theology laid out in Romans was developed by Paul himself and how much he might have learned from the apostles early in his missionary career. In 2nd Peter, the apostle indicates that the content of Paul's letters are wisdom given to Paul by God, which meshes with Paul's own explanation in the first chapter of Galatians.

Paul's letter to the Romans is most famously known for this theology (which means the study of God). In it, Paul brings out the topics of election, faith, justification, righteousness, and salvation to name a few. At first reading, and even after several readings, most will sympathize with the sentiments of Peter quoted above. These concepts have been studied, debated, and argued over since the time he wrote them. These disagreements have led to the splitting of many churches over the years which would certainly break the heart of Paul, Peter, and all the members of this brave early church. As interesting as the fine points of these theological differences are to contemplate and debate, it is important to take note that few of these differences should have any impact on the day to day decisions we make in our daily Christian walk. Paul's goal in writing this letter was not to simply convey a rational explanation of theology, but rather to help us understand God's grace enough so that we would be motivated to more completely accept it and more faithfully respond to it.

As you read Romans, don't miss the fact that his words contain within them this desperate hope that we would learn to understand, accept, appreciate, and then share the infinitely deep love of God. Paul explained this love at different levels. In v. 13:10 he said, *Love does no wrong to a neighbor* and in v. 13:19 he wrote *"You shall not commit adultery, You shall not murder, You shall not steal, You shall not covet," and any other commandment, are summed up in this word: "You shall love your neighbor as yourself."* This by itself, though, is insufficient love due to the fact that we frequently hurt others accidentally or unintentionally. Because of this, Paul taught us not to judge one another (vv. 2:1-3) and, in Ephesians 4:32, taught us to *Be kind to one another, tenderhearted, forgiving one another, as God in Christ forgave you.* God's love though, goes even deeper than this. It is not enough for us to avoid judging each other on our differences – what we often consider faults. Paul, through the Holy Spirit, taught us to love one another *because* of our uniqueness. In chapter 12 he wrote: *we, though many, are one body in Christ, and individually members one of another,* and *Bless those who persecute you; bless and do not curse them. Rejoice with those who rejoice, weep with those who weep. Live in harmony with one another. Do not be haughty, but associate with the lowly.* There is an additional depth of love that can be discerned from a study of Romans, one that Paul didn't write, but that he made evident *by* his writing. It is clear that Paul not only put effort into studying the scriptures, he put tremendous effort into learning *how* to share the gospel in an amazingly effective manner.

Reading Romans, it is clear that Paul thought carefully about his target audience. His writing does more than simply share Christian wisdom and a rational explanation of the faith: he structured his words to bring this audience through an emotional roller-coaster. Each new thought either built upon or tempered the emotional response of the previous thought. His words engaged the mind, the heart, and the soul of his early audience. Paul loved both the Jews and Gentiles of the day so much that he took time to learn *how* to convey this love in a manner that could be understood, accepted, and appreciated. Paul put his all into sharing the love that Christ shared with him. This is a message that every student of Romans should learn.

EARLY HISTORY OF THE CHURCH OF ROME

There are limited historical descriptions of life in Rome for Jews explicitly, however, there were a number of ancient historians, writers, and philosophers who left writings that tangentially provide insight into the life and hardships faced by these immigrants to Rome's capital city. When setting out to study Paul's letter, this insight is helpful in understanding the mindset of Paul's initial audience.

The first measurable population of Jews came to Rome in the 1st and 2nd centuries BC as slaves and merchants. These Jews were Greek speaking and poor. The Jews were generally tolerated in Rome and, in fact, some legal concession where made to allow them to practice their unique religion.

In 142 BC, during the time of the Jewish revolt against Greek rule, Hasmonean prince and high priest Simon Maccabee (known as *Thassi* in 1 Maccabees 2:2) sent envoys to Rome. Three years later, Valerius Maximus, a Roman author, records: *The Jews had tried to corrupt Roman values with their cult of [Yahweh], so the praetor forced them go to back to their home.* This provides interesting evidence that Romans, even at this early date, had an attraction to God's ways. Although it is recorded here that the Jews went home, they continued to have a presence in Rome in the years ahead.

In 59 BC, the Roman philosopher Cicero documented his sentiment of the Jews of the day: *You know what a big crowd it is, how they stick together, how influential they are in informal assemblies… every year it was customary to send gold to Jerusalem on the order of the Jews from Italy and from all our provinces.* These words seem to carry some of the same feelings of suspicion and resentment heard in pre-war Germany.

Hyrcanus, a leader of the Jews in Israel, supported Julius Caesar in his fight against Pompey. The historian Josephus records (Antiquities of the Jews Book XIV, Chapter 2) a series of proclamations made by Julius Caesar (46-44 BC) in appreciation for Hyrcanus's support: *Julius Caius, praetor [consul] of Rome, to the magistrates, senate, and people of the Parians, sendeth greeting. The Jews of Delos, and some other Jews that sojourn there, in the presence of your ambassadors, signified to us, that, by a decree of yours, you forbid them to make use of the customs of their forefathers, and their way of sacred worship. Now it does not please me that such decrees should be made against our friends and confederates, whereby they are forbidden to live according to their own customs, or to bring in contributions for common suppers and holy festivals, while they are not forbidden so to do even at Rome itself; for even Caius Caesar, our imperator and consul, in that decree wherein he forbade the Bacchanal rioters to meet in the city, did yet permit these Jews, and these only, both to bring in their contributions, and to make their common suppers. Accordingly, when I forbid other Bacchanal rioters, I permit these Jews to gather themselves together, according to the customs and laws of their forefathers, and to persist therein. It will be therefore good for you, that if you have made any decree against these our friends and confederates, to abrogate the same, by reason of their virtue and kind disposition towards us.*

The Romans did not understand a religion that had no physical statues of its God and considered them superstitious. However, they recognized and respected the fierceness and zeal the Jews had for their religion and the extent that they would go to defend it. The above proclamation gave Jews a unique status in the empire.

Under Augustus Caesar (27 BC-14 AD), the Jewish philosopher Philo provides a description of Jews in Rome: *The great section of Rome on the other side of the Tiber is occupied and inhabited by Jews, most of whom were Roman citizens emancipated. For having been brought as captives to Italy they were liberated by their owners and were not forced to violate any of their native institutions.... . They have houses of prayer and meet together in them, particularly on the sacred Sabbaths when they receive as a body of training in their ancestral philosophy ... They collect money for sacred purposes from their first-fruits and send them to Jerusalem by persons who would offer the sacrifices.* Paul makes a reference to this same practice of giving in Rom. 15:25-27.

After Augustus, the fortunes of the Jews in Rome declined. In 19 AD, Emperor Tiberius ordered that four thousand Jews, of suitable age, be sent out of the city and, as Tacitus, a Roman Senator and Historian, chronicles, *...be shipped to Sardinia and there be employed in suppressing brigandage.* In his writings, Tacitus describes the Jewish population as being the descendents of former slaves, brought to Rome, but now freed, within Rome, they were known as *libertini.*

The Roman historian Cassius Dio, describing events variously dated 41 AD or 49 AD during the reign of Claudius, writes: *As for the Jews, who had again increased so greatly that by reason of their multitude it would have been hard without raising a tumult to bar them from the city, he did not drive them out, but ordered them, while continuing their traditional mode of life, not to hold meetings.* The Roman Historian Suetonius, writing about this same period, reports: *Since the Jews constantly made disturbances at the instigation of Chrestus, he expelled them from Rome.* These events were just a few short years after the persecution of the church in Jerusalem began (32 AD – see Acts 8:1), from which believers where scattered to spread the gospel of Jesus throughout the empire, likely including the synagogues in Rome. Many speculate that *Chrestus* was a misspelling of *Christ* and the conflicts were a result of Jewish reaction to the preaching of the gospel of Jesus in the city. In Acts 18:2, Luke makes reference to these same events: *And he found a Jew named Aquila, a native of Pontus, recently come from Italy with his wife Priscilla, because Claudius had commanded all the Jews to leave Rome.*

Paul's letter to the church in Rome was written in ~58 AD, four years after Nero succeeded Claudius as Caesar. Early in Nero's reign, he appeared to hold no animosity towards the Jews, and in fact, his wife, Poppaea Sabina, appeared to have great sympathy for the Jews. These were uncertain times, however, for the faithful in Rome. A few short years after Paul's letter, in 64 AD, it is apparent that Christian's status as a sect of Judaism was over as the persecution of the Christians under Nero began in earnest. Of these events, Tacitus writes: *Therefore, to stop the rumor [that he had set Rome on fire], he [Emperor Nero] falsely charged with guilt, and punished with the most fearful tortures, the persons commonly called Christians, who were [generally] hated for their enormities. Christus, the founder of that name, was put to death as a criminal by Pontius Pilate, procurator of Judea, in the reign of Tiberius, but the pernicious superstition - repressed for a time, broke out yet again, not only through Judea, - where the mischief originated, but through the city of Rome also, whither all things horrible and disgraceful flow from all quarters, as to a common receptacle, and where they are encouraged. Accordingly first those were arrested who confessed they were Christians; next on their information, a vast multitude were convicted, not so much on the charge of burning the city, as of "hating the human race."*

The society that these Jews lived in was similar in some ways, but quite different in most ways, to our own. Free Roman society was comprised of a number of distinct classes. The wealthiest class, the *senatores*, were by far the wealthiest citizens of Rome. These included Senators and their families. To qualify as a Senator you had to demonstrate that you had one million *Sestertius*, in other words, your wealth was equivalent to approximately 1000 times more than a typical worker's annual wage. The *oro equester* class was next in rank. To qualify for this status, you had to demonstrate a wealth of 400,000 *Sestertius* and be at least the second generation free (non-slave) citizen. All other citizens of free birth where *plebs*. The historian Tacitus divided the plebs into *populus integer* (respectable populace) and *pebs sordida* (shabby people). The former where those able to provide for themselves (not to the extent of a *middle* class in our society - Rome had no *middle* class), while the latter where those that survived on the *dole*, a daily grain allowance equivalent to about one meal.

A citizen's rights, punishments, and economic opportunities were determined by their class and members of the upper classes wore specific clothing which identified their elite status for all to see. Those born into families which were not members of these elite classes had almost no chance of ever obtaining the economic hope and legal protections of the elite. For the people living at the time, Paul's proclamation that the faithful are children and heirs of God (v. 8:16) would have held deeper meaning than it does for those of us living in free democratic societies today.

Rome was a crowded city, to the point that only foot traffic was allowed on the streets during daytime hours. Varying estimates put the city population at the time or Paul's letter at around one million with a very small percentage being in the *senatores* and *oro equester* classes, up to 50% being slave, and the rest of the population *plebs*. Being the center of the Roman empire, the city had a significant foreign population, drawn by business opportunities or brought forcibly as slaves.

These slaves had no status in Roman society, they were property, not persons. People could find themselves enslaved through conflict, debt, piracy, or as punishment for crimes; slavery was therefore, quite multi-cultural. Criminal slaves could be sent to the mines where they were condemned to work until they died. The Roman empire had significant agricultural production requiring large numbers of slaves to work the farms.

Within the Roman system, however, it was possible (but not necessarily common) for slaves to acquire property, own other slaves themselves and, for those lucky enough, to purchase their freedom. There was an unusual mutual obligation established between freed slaves and their former masters. The masters became the *patrons* of their former slaves, while the slaves became the *client* of their former master and family. Educated slaves served in a variety of jobs for their masters and slaves of the Emperor even had authority over Roman citizens. Slaves of wealthier families could find that their life was better than those of the free, but poor, population of Rome.

It is interesting to note that the power structure of Roman society was quite different than that of modern democracies. In democracies, citizens seek to obtain government services through bureaucracies that are designed to provide these services impartially. In Roman society, this was not the case, rather, services and favors where exchanged through a social web of *patronage.* In this model, those of higher status served as *patrons* and would freely bestow a favor, provide some gift, or perform a service, such as a legal defense, to a *client* that the client was unable to provide for themselves. The client then would be obligated to support and serve their patron as needed. The support provided may include the provision of goods or services as the client was able but, more importantly, the client would ascribe honor to their patron and other electoral support such as personal testimonies. Once the patron/client relationship was established, these mutual obligations of support continued. In order to expand their powerbase or govern effectively, it was essential for a Roman citizen to establish and grow their client network. An understanding of this principal helps explain the parable of the shrewd manager, in Luke 16:1-13, where the manager not only secured friends for himself, but expanded his master's powerbase by obligating the debtors as clients of his master. As the Roman society was imbued with this notion of the patron/client relationship, it is hard to imagine that these ideas would not color their perception of Jesus' free gift of salvation. Paul, always ready to leverage cultural ideas to explain spiritual ones, uses this notion of obligation, in v.15:1, to motivate us to serve Christ by serving others.

As in our own cities, the wealthy lived in the better neighborhoods in beautiful villas while those less fortunate lived in crowded neighborhood apartments. There were a significant number of Jews living in Rome (some estimate up to 50,000), and due to their unique practices and dietary laws, they lived together in a number of distinct Jewish neighborhoods and within these neighborhoods their existed a number of synagogues. The Jews of the neighborhood shared life together and ate meals together. As mentioned above, it was customary to collect money and send it to Jerusalem. Some archaeological evidence suggests that synagogues tended to cater to different classes of people. In other words, some synagogues attracted wealthier members while other synagogues attracted the less wealthy. Again, not very different from what can be found in our own churches today.

With this understanding of Jewish society in Rome, some parts of Paul's letter can take on new meaning. As we learned above, the spread of the gospel caused such disturbance in Rome that Claudius banned the Jews from meeting and then expelled them from the city. In their absence, the gentile Christians continued the faith, forming any number of tight-knit home churches where they could meet together discreetly. These all-gentile churches would likely be free of much of the Jewish traditions. As the Jews slowly returned to Rome, it is easy to surmise that those Jews who put their faith in Christ were no longer welcome in the Jewish neighborhoods and so likely formed their own home-based churches. Life for these returning Jewish Christians would have been difficult. Not only were they separated from their fellow Jews, those of the faith that still held to the Jewish traditions would have lost their access to the kosher shops in the Jewish neighborhoods. Paul's mention, in Romans 14:2, of people that eat only vegetables, may be a reference to this situation. Much of this is speculation, but it fits both the tone and substance of Paul's letter as well as our own understanding of human nature.

At the time Paul wrote *Romans*, we see that there was no single church in Rome, but rather multiple gatherings in the homes of the believers, likely segregated by both heritage and social status. Due to this situation, there was no central leadership or teaching authority amongst the Christians to help keep them focused on the truth. The New Testament makes references to the church in Jerusalem, the church in Ephesus, the church in Smyrna, and the church in Pergamum, but no reference to the church in Rome. Rather, Romans 16:5 records *Greet also the church in their house.* It is no wonder that Paul felt compelled to reach out to the Romans, and compelled to write the powerful words contained in his letter. As we reflect on the situation in our own cities and churches, it is no wonder that the Lord acted to preserve these words for our benefit as well.

As you proceed forward with each chapter of Romans, think about the Roman culture of the day and take the time to put yourself in the shoes of the various people in Paul's target audience. Ask yourself: *If I were a Roman slave, what would my perspective be? If I were a free Roman citizen, what would my perspective be? If I were a Jew, recently returned to Rome, what would my perspective be?* Performing this exercise may help to shed additional light on these passages. Of course Paul's letters, guided as they were by the Holy Spirit, are timeless and so after considering the passages from the perspective of those early Christians, it is important to ask: *Given my own perspective of life, what does this passage mean to me?*

ROMANS 1 - 3:20

By the time Paul wrote this letter to the Romans (dated ~58 AD), he had been spreading the gospel of Christ for close to 25 years. In the course of this time he had preached to Jews, to Gentiles, and frequently both at the same time. He knew the questions, the doubts, the cultural challenges, the political challenges, the personality challenges, and most importantly, the theological challenges faced by these early churches. Because of the many friends Paul had in Rome (which he mentions at the end of his letter), it was likely that he had an understanding of the particular state of the church at this time. Paul's reputation as a brilliant, tireless (and to some, troublesome), evangelist of the faith was known throughout the empire, as were the stories of the various miracles he had performed. Paul almost certainly anticipated that when his letter finally reached the churches at Rome that the disciples would be gathered together so that the letter could be read aloud to a group of believers hungry for any words this man would share.

In the first few chapters of Romans, we see that Paul takes advantage of his reputation to hit them hard, right at the heart of some issues which he doubtless knew were crippling the church. What makes the study of this letter so powerful, is that these same issues can still cripple us today. The first few chapters help us to dig deep within ourselves so that we understand that truly, we need Christ.

1) Paul's introduction does three things:
   a) Establishes his own credentials
   b) Establishes Jesus' credentials.
   c) Presents a scripturally correct view of the gospel.
   Why did he start off this way? What tone is he setting?

2) In v. 1:5, Paul talks about the *obedience of faith* (NIV translates this as *the obedience that comes from faith*), and in v. 1:6 he reminds them that they belong to Christ (and therefore, should be obedient to Him). What is the *obedience of faith*? What were the Jews obedient to?

3) Much of the letter to the Romans is targeted at correcting some major problems he either knows, or assumes, are occurring in the church at Rome. Prior to delving into these issues, Paul, in v. 1:8, assigns attributes to the people of the church. This is a common motivational technique of Paul's (see 1 Cor.1:5, Col 1:3, 2 Cor.9:1) – he knows that people have a tendency to want to live up to the positive attributes that have been assigned to them. This verse also begins the first layer of a *criticism sandwich*, in which harsh criticism is sandwiched in between positive, uplifting words. Why does Paul go through the trouble of using these ploys? It is clear that Paul put time into studying the scriptures and clearly put time into sharing the gospel. Do you think he also put time into teaching himself how to more effectively relate to other people? Was this investment worth it to Paul? Would it be worth it to you?

4) Paul shares, as someone also of strong faith, that he prays, without ceasing for the members of the church in Rome. As these members heard his words for the first time, they would naturally (but silently) compare their own prayer life to Paul's. How do you think this comparison went? How does it go with you? How frequently do you pray for the people you know in life? Your family? Neighbors? Co-workers? What does the quality of prayer life indicate about the true depth and maturity of faith?

5) In v. 1:14 Paul says he is *under obligation*. Why does he feel *obligated* (Acts 9:15-16, Rom. 15:1, 2 Tim. 2:24-26)?

6) Paul opens the thematic statement of his letter, in v. 1:16, by saying that he is not ashamed of the gospel. Why would someone, at that time, feel a sense of shame about the gospel? In our current society, people with faith can be viewed as superstitious, unable to cope with "reality", or simply stupid. Have you ever felt ashamed or embarrassed to share your faith? If so, what is the root cause of that shame?

7) It is said that Isaac Newton first discovered gravity by noticing an apple falling from a tree. Is God discoverable through observation of the world (vv. 1:18-19)? In what ways do you perceive God in the world around you? Many other religions have appeared over the course of human history, many espousing similar ethical teachings as those contained in the Law of God and those shared by Jesus. Would Paul say that it is surprising that others would have deduced these precepts?

8) In the animal kingdom, many animals display "beauty" to attract mates. In fact, recent studies in human psychology have shown a correlation between our sense of beauty and a persons reproductive fitness (e.g. we subconsciously evaluate things like facial symmetry, hip-to-waist ratios, and even the scent of compatible antibodies. All of which, are related to reproductive health). From a scientific, Darwinian point of view, detecting beauty in a mate serves a logical purpose. Humans, however, also see beauty in natural things, such as sunsets, and the way light can filter softly through a wooded forest. What is the Darwinian purpose in this? Why might we have this sense of beauty and majesty in these things?

9) In v. 1:24, Paul writes that *God gave them up in the lusts of their*

hearts... What does this mean that *God gave them up*? Have you seen instances in our society where people used to be aware of shame and guilt, but now no longer have that feeling? Perhaps in casual sexual relationships, corporate greed, or gluttony? Are there any areas in your life where God has given you up to your desires? How would you know? Are there any "tools" available to the Christian to help with this?

10) When you have succumbed to your own evil desires, how did you feel afterwards? Did you pay a price for it? Have these behaviors ever led you to unfulfilled relationships, a sense that you are lacking in compassion, feelings of loneliness, boredom, or general loss of fulfillment or meaning in life?

11) In comparison with the previous question, have you ever done something selfless, acting with great compassion for someone else? How did this make you feel afterwards?

12) Is approving of sin less of a sin then the sin itself (v. 1:32, Isa. 5:20)? Do we have an obligation, within our society, to call sin a sin, or is it acceptable to stay silent? In our work or neighborhood environments, how do you avoid silently approving of sin, while at the same time, avoid alienation so that you can continue to demonstrate God's love and grace?

13) In vv. 1:28-31, Paul lays out a litany of sins (see also Gal. 5:19-21). How many of these are *actions* and how many are *attitudes*? How does he rank these (see v. 1.32, James 2:10-14). Which of these sins, mentioned in vv. 1:28-31, have you been guilty of, to any degree, within the past five years? Is it possible that God has, in some way, given you over to a debased mind so that you do not acknowledge him? How would you know?

14) In what ways have you sensed God's kindness, tolerance, and patience (v. 2:4)? Do you believe that kindness, as expressed through you, could help lead others to repentance? Do you keep this in mind in your daily interactions with people in need of repentance?

15) Do you have an unrepentant heart (v. 2:5)? If so, what is the root cause of your stubbornness?

16) Two contrasting sequences are presented in v. 2-7 and v. 2-8. What are they? v. 2-8 uses the phrase *do not obey the truth* (translated in NIV as *reject the truth*). What is *truth* and what would it mean to obey it?

17) Verses 2:14-15, 2:26, as well as 1:20, discuss our ability to be aware of, and respond to, God's laws without necessarily having formal training in the law of Moses or the teachings of Jesus. Is it possible for someone to have a restored relationship with God by responding in faith to these laws written on their heart, without being formally introduced to Christianity? (For discussion, see also Mat. 7:7, 28:16-20, John 3:16.) Is it possible to have a restored relationship with God if you actually study His words and the scripture, but then reject Him?

18) Is it OK to obey what is written on your heart but reject Jesus? How would a parent feel if their child was polite, doing well in school, but refused to speak to them?

19) Do you have thoughts that both accuse and defend you (v. 2:15)? Which do you prefer to listen to? Which have steered you right most often? Have you taught yourself the discipline to control your destructive thoughts? If so, how did you do it?

20) In the book of Acts (Acts 15:1) and Paul's letter to the Galatians (Gal. 2:4), we learn about the Judaizers who believed Jesus was the Messiah, but still believed in the law. What were the Jews waiting for the Messiah to do for them (Ps. 72:11, Mic. 4)? Did they, because of their Jewish heritage, feel that they already had an "in" with *their* Messiah?

21) In your experience, when two groups of people co-exist, but one group feels especially privileged, what tends to happen?

22) Paul tells the Jews that God's name has been blasphemed amongst the Gentiles because of them. Can wisdom be extracted from vv. 2:17-29 and applied to our situation today? Is God's name blasphemed because of actions Christians take? Have you ever tried to reach out to a non-believer only to have them reject you because they see Christians as unkind, hateful, or hypocritical? What gave them that impression? Are you always conscience of the impression you are making through your everyday words and actions?

23) As this letter of Paul's was read aloud, for the first time, to the churches in Rome, how do you think the Jews were feeling up through chapter two? Did the Jews of the day, as a group, tend to be quiet, stoic, and thoughtful, or vibrantly emotional (see Acts 22, particularly vv. 22:22-23)? What do you think their internal, visceral, reaction might be? Do you tend to listen much after you've been attacked?

24) In vv. 3:1-2, Paul tones down his letter and de-escalates the emotional level a bit. Can you perceive how Paul communicates both intellectually and emotionally with this complex target audience? When you are reaching out to others, do you put this much thought into *how* you reach out to them?

25) The oracles of God (v. 3:2) refer to the promises that God made to the Jews. Read Ex. 19:3-6,24:3. How would you summarize these promises? Did the Israelites promise to be faithful? If the Lord warns you about making an oath in his name (Lev. 19:12), how seriously do you think he takes the oath made to him personally?

26) In v. 3:3, Paul asks, rhetorically, *what if some where faithless?* After the Jews made their oath to God, Moses led them in the desert for 40 years. What were Moses' thoughts on the Israelites ability to remain faithful (Deut. 31:24-29)?

27) What does God say about his own faithfulness (Duet. 4:25-31)?

28) Read the words of God spoken to the prophet Isaiah, as recorded in Isaiah 49, particularly, Isa. 49:7. The 2nd half of v. 3:3 asks if our faithlessness nullifies God's faithfulness. How would you have answered the question? Do we deserve God's faith? Why do you think God remains faithful, even though we don't?

29) In v. 3:5, Paul introduces a startling concept: God does not believe that we can appreciate his goodness without allowing us to experience life without his goodness. Has God done this before (see v. 1:24, Jer. 22:6-9, Ezra 9:6-8, and in particular, Gen. 3:11-14)? Does v. 3:5 imply that God made us unrighteous?

30) Have you ever done evil that good may come? Have you ever

told a white lie? Manipulated people or events to gain power and status so that you could be in a position to do good things? What does v. 3:8 have to say about this?

31) In Paul's quotations of Psalms & Isaiah (vv. 3:10-18), he highlights an important definition of works. What kind of works is referred to in v. 3:13? When you evaluate yourself in terms of the good works you do, do you consider first, and foremost, the words that you speak or don't speak? Look in a concordance and find all the verses that contain the words *encourage, tongue, lips, throat, mouth, words,* etc. From this exercise, how important would you say that God considers the words we speak? How much attention do you give to the words you speak?

The few short verses of Romans vv. 3:18-20 delve into some of the core concepts of God's grand plan for His relationship with us: concepts that can be elusive to grasp. Genesis 2 teaches us that God created Adam and lived in harmony with him. When man ate the fruit of the tree of knowledge of good and evil his relationship was severed. Later, God gave the Israelites His law explicitly, although Paul, in the early chapters of Romans, teaches us that all men are accountable to His law because it has been made plain to us. Paul now teaches us that God demands justice and

Johnny and the Lollipop

Little Johnny walked home from his first day of kindergarten. As he passed through town, all alone for the first time, he decided to stop in at the local pharmacy to say hello to Mr. Beal, the shop owner. After sharing his excitement of the day, he took a lollipop from a dish on the counter and headed on home: it was a better lollipop than those at the barbershop – it had a nice chocolate center. So this, then, became Johnny's habit each afternoon: exchanging a few words with Mr. Beal, and grabbing a tasty lollipop on the way out the door.

After a few weeks of this, Johnny invited a friend home after school and so they both popped in to say hello to the pharmacist, and, as usual, Johnny grabbed a lollipop on the way out. As they headed to the door though, his friend, with an expression of horror etched across his face, grabbed Johnny by the coat and whispered into his ear: "Johnny, you can't just walk out with that, you didn't pay for it yet!" Johnny turned, his gaze following his friends outstretched arm up to his hand and finger which was pointing to the side of the lollipop jar. His eyes read for the first time: "Lollipops 5¢ each". Dumbstruck, Johnny turned his gaze up to Mr. Beal who looked back at him over his half-round spectacles. Mr. Beal gave just a hint of a smile, then turned back to his work saying simply, "see you tomorrow Johnny."

accountability for the trespass against the law. And finally, we know that He sent His son, Jesus, to incur the wrath and punishment for our sins so that we can have a restored relationship with God, a relationship like Adam started out with. This begs the question, wouldn't it have been simpler if God just never planted that tree of the knowledge of good and evil? If He knew we could never obey His law, why give it to us in the first place? If He was just going to forgive us, why did He need to send his son to the cross? Why didn't he just forget about our sins? To help understand one aspect of this, consider the story of Johnny and the Lollipop in the sidebar.

32) Mr. Beal's love of Johnny, and his expression of grace and

forgiveness existed before the friend stopped by; Johnny was simply not aware of it. After the incident, do you think Johnny's affection was deeper for Mr. Beal than it would have been otherwise? Prior to this incident, Johnny would likely have considered Mr. Beal just another nice adult. Afterward, do you think Johnny would have had a richer understanding of Mr. Beal's character and an increased sense of loyalty to this relationship? That is, if someone on the schoolyard tried to say bad things about Mr. Beal, do you think Johnny would be more inclined to defend him? Did Johnny's knowledge of Mr. Beal's grace and forgiveness change the relationship? In the same way, can you see how the depth, quality, and maturity of our relationship with God may be deeper now than was otherwise possible with God and Adam in the garden of Eden?

33) What is the purpose of the Law? Note that Gal. 3:24 tells us that *...the law was our guardian until Christ came..* The Greek word used for guardian in this verse is *Paidagogos.* At the time, *Paidagogos* referred to a tutor or guardian, typically a slave, that was put in charge of teaching morals and supervising the life of boys in the upper classes of society.

34) In v. 13:10, Paul writes: *Love does no wrong to a neighbor; therefore love is the fulfilling of the law.* Without knowing the law, is it possible to avoid hurting others or hurting God unintentionally?

35) Does God view justice as important and necessary (vv. 16:19-20, Ps. 37:28, Prov. 21:16, Mic. 6:8)? Do you understand why God's justice was necessary (Prov. 28:5)?

ROMANS 3:21-7

Starting with verse 3:21, Paul begins a challenging explanation of how we can become right with God through our faith in Jesus. For the Jewish followers of the day, these concepts were difficult and sometimes confrontational because Paul injects new, revelatory, interpretations of the scriptures for which they would have been intimately familiar and, in doing so, forces these Israelites to question and re-think all that they thought they knew. In the early years of his ministry, Paul found himself being stoned when he made his arguments with insufficient delicacy. His explanations in the next few chapters use a multi-layered approach to making his points, drawing from key aspects of the Jewish traditions and doing so in a typically confident, yet reverent manner.

The starting point of Paul's arguments is our need to have faith in Jesus. Paul, as well as the other New Testament writers, frequently talk about having *faith* in Jesus (v. 1:22), but what does it mean to have faith? To get a relatable view of faith, consider Ed and Kate, a couple that had been married for over 40 years. Each evening Kate prepared dinner for her husband, and after each dinner, Ed always commented on what a wonderful meal it was. Neither doubted that they would be there for each other. They had faith in one another; a faith that combined the obvious believe that each would be there at dinner, with trust that they would serve each other with loving tenderness. The faith that the New Testament writers talk about encompasses these qualities: belief, trust, a willingness to accept the service and affection of the other, and a willingness to serve one another. These are some of the key characteristics of a vibrant relationship with Christ.

The Righteousness of God

The original Greek word translated in Rom. 3:22 as *righteous* is *dikaiosune*. Significant research has been done on the original intended meaning of this word so that Paul's letters can be more clearly understood. In the 5th century BC, a historian named Herodotus used *dikaiosune* as a legal term referring to the clear objective, and fair thinking of a judge when determining what each of the parties before him is due. The term was also used to describe the adjustment made in the lives of the parties involved to conform to this fair judgment. The phrase *righteousness of God* (translated as *righteousness from God* in the NIV) carries several connotations, but essentially refers to His perfect and fair judgment. When we are righteous, we are (or have been found to be) conforming to His judgment and therefore are in a condition or state that is acceptable and approved by God.

Referring to 2 Cor. 5:21, some scholars argue that when used in the phrase *become the righteousness of God*, Paul is conveying the idea that God is fulfilling His promises by using us as agents to convey His fair and perfect judgments to others so that they might become conformant to them as well.

---

1) In v. 3:22, Paul describes a righteousness of God *for all who believe*. Believe in what? Often people think they believe something, but when put to the test, their belief falters. What evidence is their that you have the type of belief that Paul is talking about (see James 2:19-23)? Read Mark 9:24. Have you ever felt like this father? Was Jesus willing to accept this level of belief?

2) Have you ever been in a situation where someone else willingly took the blame for you for breaking a rule? Did you learn any lessons from the rule, even though you were not the one punished? Did it have a different feel to it than if you never got caught? Did you feel as though you were in debt to the person who took the blame for you?

3) People frequently do good works in order to please God. What things can we do to satisfy God's justice and redeem ourselves from the sins we have committed? What type of sacrifice, or payment, does God find satisfactory (Ex. 12:5-7, Lev. 4:1-4)? Why did the sacrifice have to be Christ (1 Pet. 1:19)?

4) In v. 3:25, Paul mentions God's divine forbearance. For perspective, note that God "rebooted" man's presence on earth with Noah (Gen. 5), who lived, according to Biblical calculations, around 5000 BC. Why do you think God might have delayed justice for so many centuries when man has clearly been sinning all along? What technological and physical infrastructure would be needed for apostles to spread the message of His grace throughout the whole earth?

5) Christians frequently share with each other the good things they are doing, but does boasting about these things get us any closer to God (v. 3:27)? Should we keep silent about these things? What legitimate purpose could there be in boasting (2 Cor. 11:21-12:10)?

6) In what way is the law upheld (v. 3:31)?

7) In v. 4:3, Paul quotes Moses, as he wrote about Abraham's relationship with God (Gen. 15). The Hebrew word Moses used for *believed* was *'aman*, which means *to confirm and affirm* and was frequently used in the context of contracts or covenants. In Gen. 15:6, what was Abraham confirming and affirming? What did God demand of Abraham before promising to make his offspring numerous as the stars? What did he demand of Abraham before declaring him righteous? What did God demand of us before promising a new covenant (Luke 22:20, 1 Cor. 11:25)? What does he demand of us before declaring us righteous?

8) Paul quotes King David's Psalm 32 in vv. 4:7-8. What actions did David take to prepare himself for God's Grace (Ps. 32:5-7)? How does Jesus message compare with David's (Luke 13:3-5)?

9) The Jews considered the fact that they where "children of Abraham" something special – something that gave them unique status in God's eyes. In Romans 4, Paul challenges this. To understand Paul's challenge, it is insightful to consider Jesus' own lineage. In Math. 1:5, we learn Jesus descended from Ruth, a woman who's story is documented in the book of Ruth. In Ruth 1:4, we learn that Ruth was a Moabite, not an Israelite. Does it sound like God's blessing extended to Ruth? Do you think, in His eyes, she became an Israelite? What was it about Ruth that would cause God to see her as a child of Abraham (Ruth 1:15-16)? Was Ruth accepting Naomi because of her love of God, or was she accepting God because of her love of Naomi? Was Ruth sacrificing anything to make this commitment to Naomi? What does God seem to be considering when He counts someone as a child of Abraham, is it simply genetic heritage, or something else? What was Jesus thoughts on being children of Abraham (Mat. 3:9)?

10) Abraham received the sign of circumcision as a seal of the

righteousness accorded to him because of his faith. The Greek word translated as *seal* is *Sphragis*, which refers to the type of seal pressed onto a document or paper by a signet ring which authenticates it as belonging to, or endorsed by the ring's owner. Has God also put a seal on the uncircumcised faithful (1 Cor. 1:22)? What guarantee did he leave us?

11) In v. 4:15, Paul again indicates that where there is no law, there is no wrath. Consider again the story of Johnny and the lollipop. Before Johnny knew that Mr. Beal charged for the lollipops, did Mr. Beal think of Johnny as stealing? Was he angry? If, however, Johnny continued to take lollipops, knowing that he was stealing, would Mr. Beal's attitude be different?

12) Paul's words can sometimes be a challenge because he speaks of things like life and death in a spiritual sense rather than a physical sense. In v. 4:16, is the offspring that Paul talks about Abraham's genetic offspring, or spiritual offspring?

13) Did Abraham always have a strong faith, or did his faith change over time (vv. 4:20-21)? Should your faith remain constant once you accept Jesus as your savior?

14) In v. 4:23, Paul makes the pronouncement that God's words to Abraham apply to us as well. Do you think that this is a justifiable argument? Why?

15) In v. 5:1, Paul explains that our faith provides peace with God as well as access to his grace (see also Eph. 2:18, 3:12). How do you take advantage of this access?

16) In chapters 1-4, Paul has explained how God declares us as righteous through our faith. In v. 5:2, he uses the word "hope" which implies that we are waiting for something in the future.

Does this mean that righteousness is not the end goal of the Christian? If not, what else is there (1: Pet. 1:9, Rom. 8:18-23)?

17) The Greek word translated as glory, in v. 5:2, is *doxa*. *Doxa* has nuanced meanings and is variously translated as glory, glorious, honor, praise, dignity, and worship. It's definition includes the concept of evaluation with a resulting judgment of magnificence. Is its usage in v. 5:2 referring to the glory that we are to obtain, the glory of God, or something else (1 Pet. 6:7, Rom. 8:18,21)?

18) What types of trials and hardships might have afflicted the Christians in the churches of Rome at the time? What types of hardships and challenges do we face today? Did Paul know what it means to suffer for Christ (2 Cor. 11:25)? Did the other apostle writers agree with the philosophy expressed in vv. 5:3-5 by Paul (1 Pet. 6, James 1:2-4)? Have you had difficulty maintaining an attitude of joy at your own sufferings? How can you move your way of thinking to that of the apostles?

19) As a means of growing closer to Christ, some people have deliberately inflicted suffering on themselves. This has taken different forms: anything from beating ones self with chains or whips, to avoiding foods that are otherwise enjoyable. Do these verses imply that Christians should deliberately cause themselves suffering or, is it referring to the unavoidable suffering that Christians may endure as a result of their faith and the unavoidable hardships of this fallen world?

20) In v. 5:9, Paul indicates that even after putting our faith in Jesus and being justified by this faith, we have a continuing need of salvation. In what ways does this continuing salvation manifest itself? Who's responsibility is it to maintain the continuing salvation (v. 12:2, 2 Cor. 4:16)?

21) Can we lose our salvation (Acts 5:1-11, James 5:19-20, vv. 11:20-21)? Note: There is disagreement among theologians on this topic – some make valid arguments that once God has placed his seal on us, it implies and irrevocable salvation (v. 11:29). However, is their any wisdom in ignoring God and not making a deliberate attempt to grow in faith and knowledge of him after accepting Jesus? Is failing to do so a form of rejection?

22) In v. 5:12, Paul again is speaking in spiritual terms. When Paul speaks of *death* in these passages, what do you think he is referring to? When he speaks of *life*, what *life* is he referring to?

23) Is the free gift of God automatic? What must we do to get this gift (v. 5:17)? What is the free gift (vv. 3:24, 6:23)?

24) What does it mean to reign in life? Who will reign (v. 5:17, 1 Cor. 15:20)? How long will Christ reign (1 Cor. 15:23-26, Rev. 5:10, Rev. 22:5)?

25) There are no prophetic references to a "second Adam" in the Old Testament, and, with the exception of Hosea, no mention of him at all outside of Genesis. Paul, however, uses this parallel comparison of Adam and Christ in several of his letters.

Why did he feel this comparison was necessary or useful? What objection or theological stumbling block do you believe he was trying to address?

26) In Rom. 6, Paul personifies *sin* as a literary way to make the argument that we died to sin and, therefore, are no longer a slave to sin. What does this mean? Does it mean that we will no longer sin? Does it mean that we will no longer be accountable for our sins? Does it mean that we will no longer have the desire to sin? How do your answers agree with your own personal experience?

27) How well does Paul's explanation mesh with that of Jesus Himself (John 3:1-17)?

28) In v. 6:3 Paul writes *Do you not know that all of us who have been baptized into Christ Jesus were baptized into his death?* Which seems to indicate that our baptism into Christ joins us as one spiritual being. In Eph. 5:22-33, Paul makes the analogy of the Church being the bride of the Christ and, in Math. 19:5-6, Jesus, quoting Moses, describes marriage as binding two individuals into one flesh. How does Paul's analysis compare with Jesus' own prayer for us as recorded in John 17:22-23? After marriage, does a person still struggle with their own selfish wants and desires that may be in contrast to what is good for their spouse and marriage?

29) Paul exhorts us to *Let not sin therefore reign in your mortal body, to make you obey its passions.* Does this imply that God will miraculously keep us from sinning, or will it take some effort on our part? How do sinful passions spring forth? How can you keep yourself from succumbing to them?

30) Paul uses an analogy of slavery to describe our living. Does his use of this analogy imply that we are forced to do whatever God tells us to do or that we are like puppets (v. 6:19)?

31) In v. 3:28 Paul taught that our justification is brought about by faith rather than works. Now, in v. 6:22 (see also vv. 7:4-6), we see that our *sanctification* (defined as our continuing growth in the Spirit towards purity – sometimes translated as *holiness*) is the fruit of our slavery to righteousness. Is it possible to do nothing at all and yield fruit? Does our faith alone yield fruit? In Gal. 5:22, Paul expounds on the fruits of the Spirit. Is it possible to express love, goodness, and kindness to its fullest extent without reaching out to others? Without providing service? Can you develop gentleness, faithfulness, peace, patience, and self-control without working on it? In what ways do you work on these things?

32) As a married couple lives life together, sharing the experiences of building a home, building a circle of friends, or serving together, do they grow to become more like one another? Could this same type of growth occur if they lived apart? As you serve together with the Spirit, expressing love and kindness to others, does it seem natural that you would begin to grow more pure, like the Spirit of God you are serving together with? Is sanctification something you earn through these works, or a byproduct of this relationship? In v. 6:23, Paul says that the *free gift of God is eternal life in Christ Jesus our Lord*. If you refuse to serve others and refuse to grow your heart, is it possible to accept this free gift, or does your refusal imply a rejection of the gift? If, for some reason, you don't want to share this life with God now, why do you want to be with Him later?

33) The Jews felt special because they were God's chosen people. In chapters 1-3, Paul demonstrates that the Jews behavior is no better than anyone else's. Then, in the end of chapter 3, continuing to chapter 4, Paul demonstrates that adhering to the law will never lead us to justification anyway. In Chapter 4, Paul explains that being the genetic progeny of Abraham has no value; it is the spiritual progeny of Abraham that counts. Likewise, physical circumcision has no value, only spiritual circumcision, and now, in v. 7:6, Paul declares that the Law no longer applies to the believers at all. Was it easy for the Jewish Christians of the time to accept these new concepts (Acts 11:2-3, 21:20-21, Gal. 5:1-15, Titus. 1:10-11)? Which has the ability to bring us closer to God, following the old Jewish customs, or the teachings of the Gospel and the apostles? We have all grown up with beliefs and customs and it is likely that the study of God's words challenges us in a manner similar to that in which the Jews of the day were challenged. How should we handle this challenge? Do you experience a feeling of loss or even grief when you contemplate letting go of erroneous beliefs or customs that you grew up with? Is accepting this new understanding of our relationship with God worth it? Why or why not?

34) Since placing faith in Christ, have the selfish and sinful temptations of this world disappeared? As you have grown in your relationship with Christ, have you noticed a change in the way you handle temptations?

35) Can you relate to Paul's description of the affects of the law in vv. 7:7-8? Have you ever had the desire to have something or do something just because you found out you can't or shouldn't? Have you ever seen a television commercial that takes advantage of this principle?

36) Compare Paul's words in v. 7:11, to the scriptures in Gen. 2:16-17 which reads: *And the LORD God commanded the man, saying, "You may surely eat of every tree of the garden, but of the tree of the knowledge of good and evil you shall not eat, for in the day that you eat of it you shall surely die."* Do the words of the Law provide knowledge of good and evil? What is it that dies? Are these words referring to the physical death of our bodies, or are they being used figuratively to refer to something else?

37) Some theologians have argued that once you are declared righteous by your faith, you become free of all desire to sin. However, in your own experience as a Christian, have you ever wrestled with sinful desires as Paul does in vv. 7:15-25? Have you ever wanted to do something that you knew was right and/or felt led to do, but then chickened out or found excuses not to do it? Is there any value in wallowing in guilt when you have these experiences? What would be a more appropriate

response?

ROMANS 8

In the previous chapters of Paul's letter, Paul discussed the righteousness of God and how we, as faithful followers of Christ, share in this righteousness. Since the days of the early Church, priests and scholars have been reading and analyzing these words and have developed a number of, sometimes competing, theological ideas to explain in more detail what Paul was talking about. The terms *imputed*, *imparted*, and *infused* righteousness have been used to describe some of these ideas. The danger of this study is that some seek this better understanding so that they can know what the minimum threshold is in order to "get into heaven". Having this notion misses the point of Paul's exhortations completely. In chapter 8, Paul begins to share with us the true attitude of a faithful follower.

1) What hope do we have when we find ourselves sinning against our better judgment (vv. 5:10, 7:24-25)? What should our response be (vv. 6:19, 8:5)? As we commit to being "slaves of righteousness", should we expect our sanctification to be immediate? If not, would it be reasonable to expect the kinds of struggles that Paul shares with us?

2) How do you go about setting your mind on things of the Spirit? What types of habits did the spiritual leaders use to help them (vv. 1:9-10, Ezra 7:10)?

3) In v. 8:3, Paul explains that Jesus sent his son in the *likeness* of sinful flesh. In what way was Jesus different than the rest of us (1 Peter 2:22, John 8:46, 2 Cor. 5:21, 1 John 3:5, Heb. 7:26, 9:14)?

4) What gives life (John 6:63, Rom. 8:6)? Who will get the Spirit (John 7:37-39, Acts 2:38)?

Word usage in Romans 8:18-35

The Greek word *Eido* is translated as *know* but *Eido* also can refer to things perceived. In v. 8:28, some argue that the Greek form of the word indicates that *we know because we have perceived*.

The Greek word *Ktisis* (v. 8:19) is used in the scriptures to refer to the whole of God's creation, to the act of creating, and also to refer to that which has been created. In a number of verses, the word is used to refer to the unredeemed Gentiles of the world (Mark 16:15, Col. 1:23, Heb. 4:13).

The Greek Word *Mataiotes* used in v. 8:20 has variously been translated as futility, vanity, or frustration and refers to that which is frail, depraved, and/or devoid of truth. This word is used in Eph. 4:17 and 2 Peter 2:18 to refer to the mental state of Gentiles who have not yet received the spirit of Christ.

The Hebrew word *yada* is frequently translated as *know* and implies the formation of a deep, loving, relationship as seen in Gen 4:1: *Now Adam knew Eve his wife, and she conceived and bore Cain.* Many scholars postulate Paul's use of the word *foreknew* in v. 8:29 carries this connotation.

5) In v. 8:12, Paul tells us we are debtors. Why does he think we are debtors (Col. 2:14)? In your daily walk with Christ, do you carry with you the feeling of owing a debt? Have you ever felt led to "make payments" on this debt? Is it necessary for us to do this?

6) In v. 8:17, Paul teaches that we are co-heirs of Christ. When someone becomes an heir to an estate, what privileges do they inherit? What duties do they inherit? What did Jesus inherit that we are now deemed to be co-heirs of? What privileges and duties might this imply (v. 8:17, John 21:15-17, 13:34)?

7) In describing our new relationship with God, Paul chooses to use the informal term of *Abba* (v. 8:15), which would be analogous to our current use of *Daddy*. What point was Paul trying to make? Do you view your relationship with God with this level of comfort and intimacy? Paul's reference to the word *Daddy* is certainly effective for those who have had loving and affectionate fathers. Was this the case with you? If not, how has the lack of this experience influenced your view of God? Have you ever had a relationship on earth that was characterized by the deep, selfless, compassionate type of love that God intends for us to have with one another?

8) In v. 8:17, Paul indicates that we must suffer with Christ. What provisions has God made to help us through these sufferings (John 13:34-35, 2 Cor. 1:4-5, John 14:26 - Note that in this verse, the word *helper*, is often translated as *comforter*)?

9) Why was the "creation" made subject to frustration (v. 1:24)? Who received the first fruits of the Spirit of God (Acts 1:8)? What is Paul trying to say in Romans 8:18-24? What do you think he meant when he said that glory will be revealed in us? What was Paul so excited about?

10) Who had been found worthy of righteousness prior to Christ's resurrection (vv. 4:6, 4:22)? Did God predestine that those under the old covenant would benefit from Christ's sacrifice (Heb. 9:15)? Did God go to any trouble to take care of the faithful prior to the coming of the Messiah, did he "have their back" (vv. 8:28-30)? If he was willing and able to take such good care of those who lived before the arrival of Christ, can he protect and nurture you as well (vv. 8:31-39)?

Note that some theologians don't view vv. 8:29-30 as referring to those that came before Christ, but rather interpret them to mean that God knew us each individually, and chose which of us will be called, before we are born (Jer. 1:5, Acts 17:26, Rev. 13:8.)

11) Have you ever felt a little lost in your spiritual walk – had the sense that you weren't on the right track, but didn't know what to do about it? What words of comfort does Paul share with us

(vv. 8:26-27)? Should we be anxious and upset if the God isn't acting fast enough for us?   What should our attitude be (v. 8:25)?

ROMANS 9-11

In the first eight chapters, Paul puts forth a convincing argument why both the Jews and the Gentiles within the church have been saved and declared righteous – not through following laws and traditions, but by faith in Jesus Christ alone. As the Jews of the day came to realize the truth in Paul's words, these arguments carried with them both joy and pain. Joy that their own personal relationship with the Lord had been restored, but tremendous pain in coming to realize that their family, their brothers, sisters, cousins, and neighbors, and all the loved ones that they knew and shared their rich heritage with, were destined for destruction. The pain that these early Jews felt can still be felt by people today who come to know the Lord but whose friends or family choose not to follow.

In these next few chapters, Paul empathizes with this pain and helps to answer the questions that were destined to be raised: How could this be? Why would God let this happen? Is there any hope left for Israel?

1) The story of the birth of Isaac's twin sons Esau and Jacob is told in Genesis 25. Jacob was later given the name Israel and became the father of the Israelite nation. Esau was the older son and was in line to receive God's blessing, however, in Gen. 25:34 we learn that Esau had such little regard for God's blessing that he sold this birthright to his younger son in

55

exchange for some red lentil soup. Later, in Gen. 27:41 we find that Esau plotted to kill Jacob. Esau became the father of the Edomite nation (Edom means "red" and is a reference to the color of the lentil stew). In the story of God's deliverance of the Israelites from Egypt, we learn in Numbers 20, the nation of Edom refused to allow the Israelites to pass through their land. The early books of the Bible show that the Edom nation was a continual thorn in the side of Israel. In v. 9:13, Paul quotes Mal. 1:3, a passage that, in context, refers to God's hatred of the nation of Edom. Was God's hatred arbitrary or did both Esau personally, and his nation as a whole, have an opportunity to seek God?

2) Paul indicates that Jacob, individually, was identified by God for a special purpose. The circumstances around Moses birth and early life (Ex. 2) seem to indicate that God's hand was directly involved so that he would have the skills, status, and position to fulfill God's purpose at exactly the time needed. Okne could argue the same for Paul himself. Does this indicate that God created each of us individually for a particular, specific purpose, or that God, on rare occasions, intervened in special ways to fulfill His plans for redemption?

3) Anyone who has traveled to foreign countries comes to realize that what seems fair and logical in one culture can vary greatly to that which seems fair or logical in another culture. For example, within capitalist societies, people believe that it is fair and just to provide everyone equal opportunities, however, in socialist societies, people believe that it is fair and just to provide everyone equal benefits. Have you ever felt that "God isn't nice", or "God isn't fair"? These thoughts can sometimes arise when a passage of the scripture isn't properly understood and sometimes they can arise when we evaluate God based on our own cultural idea of fairness. Romans chapter 9 provides ample opportunity for both these errors. Jesus used many parables to help people understand God's view of fairness and justice. Read Mat. 20:1-16. How, in your own words, would you describe God's idea of fairness? As we have learned, all have sinned and are unworthy of God's grace. If He chooses to show mercy to some, is that wrong? Each year you are given the opportunity to give to a multitude of charities and good causes. If you choose to give to some, but not all, is that wrong of you? If you choose to lend a hand to some people you know who are in need, but not everyone you meet that is in need, is that wrong?

4) Genesis tells the story of Jacob's son, Joseph, who was made second in command to Pharaoh and brought God's blessings to all of Egypt. Joseph brought the Israelites to Egypt where they lived for 400 years, giving the Egyptians plenty of time to learn of God's words. History tells us that the Pharaohs never came to love the Lord but instead continued in their own cult religions and, in fact, came to believe that the Pharaohs themselves were gods. Exodus tells us also that over the course of these 400 years the Egyptians came to enslave the Israelite

nation – God's people. In v. 9:17, Paul makes reference to God hardening Pharaoh's heart (Ex. 4:21, 7:3, 14:4, 14:17). Had Pharaoh already chosen a path apart from God before Moses came and performed miracles? Were these miracles an act of grace intended for the Israelite nation or intended for the Egyptian nation? When the Lord "hardened" Pharaoh's heart, was he *making* Pharaoh sinful, or was he simply *preventing* Pharaoh from responding to the miracles which were intended as an act of mercy for the Israelites (in other words, preserving the sinful state of Pharaoh's heart as it was before the miracles)?

5) In vv. 9:20-25, Paul makes reference to the words of Jeremiah the prophet (Jer. 18:1-12) (which in turn refer to man being made from the earth – Gen. 2:7). In this passage of Jeremiah, does God provide no hope for vessels made for destruction, or do the vessels have the opportunity to win God's favor? Likewise, are there things that a vessel of mercy can do to lose God's favor? Do these passages take away from God's sovereignty or simply give us a glimpse of his heart?

6) The Bible encourages us to understand God better through both the study of the scriptures and through our prayer life. Usually, we learn best by asking good questions and then

seeking the answer. In vv. 9:19-21, as in the story of Job, scripture chastises us for some questions. What is it about the questions in vv. 9:19-20 that causes chastisement? Have you ever asked God "Why have you made me like this?"

7) Paul's quotation of Hosea 2:23 in v. 9:25 is revealing of Paul's ability to extract wisdom from scripture. In the first two chapters of Hosea, we find that *Not my children* (*Lo-ammi* in Hebrew) was the name God commanded Hosea to give to his third child as a symbol of the fact that the nation of Israel had strayed so far from God that He no longer recognized the Israelites as His children. In the context of Hosea, *Not my children* clearly refers to the Israelite nation, while in Paul's quotation, he is clearly referencing Gentiles. Some scholars have interpreted Paul's quotation to imply that Christians are now the "new" Israelites while others have argued that the Holy Spirit, working through Paul, is "re-interpreting" the otherwise plain understanding of the ancient scriptures. A more straightforward view is that Paul sees an analogy between the sinful Israelites of Hosea's day and sinful people everywhere today. What wisdom and insight into the heart and nature of God was Paul picking up on from the passage of Hosea? Has Paul, in a similar fashion, extracted wisdom from the stories of Adam and Abraham? Can this idea of extracting wisdom from the scriptures be used today (from passages such as v. 2:24, for example) to help guide our own walk?

Take a moment to write down as many of the "rules" that are important in your church or in your Christian relations; use the prompts below to help.

- For your priest/pastor: What type of clothing is appropriate? What types of sermons should they give? Where should they live? What should their qualifications be?

- For your church: What type of music should they play? What day and time should services be held? Who can give communion? Who can serve communion? What type of communion elements should there be? Who should be in charge at your church, who should have the final say? Who should be allowed to teach in church? How should the church raise money? Who should be allowed to attend your church? How should the church be decorated? What should children do during services?

- For yourself: What type of clothing is appropriate for you to wear in church? Outside church? How much should you give? When should you give? How much should you serve? How long should you serve in a particular role?

8) As you review these rules listed above, would you say that these rules create opportunity for Christians to judge one another?

9) In Israel, the Pharisees took the Word of God and codified it into hundreds of specific *do's* and *don'ts* so that everyone would have a clear idea of how to be right with God. Is the list of rules noted above any different? Read v. 9:31. Where did this kind of thinking lead the Israelites? All of their codified laws are rooted in God's word. Do you think that following these laws was a bad thing to do? Why did they cause the Israelites to stumble and fail to obtain the righteousness of God? Do you argue that the rules you noted above are all rooted in God's

word? What did Paul have to say about the Israelites Law (v. 10:4)? Within any group, having an organizational structure, or agreed upon processes is useful. Is this how the rules you listed above are thought of, or are they thought of as Holy "rules"? If the latter, how are they different from the laws of the Pharisees? If we don't live by these rules, how should we live? How should we allow others to live?

10) In v. 9:32, Paul makes a reference to Psalm 118 (118:22-23). Jesus quoted this same psalm in Mat. 21:42-44. What did Jesus say the consequences of rejecting the cornerstone would be? How does Jesus prediction mesh with the overall argument Paul is making? Is it still possible for us to stumble in the same way as the Israelites did?

11) In v. 10:2, Paul bears witness to the Israelites' zeal for God. Does he truly understand them (Acts 22:1-5, Phil. 2:4-6)? Out of all the zealous Israelites, why do you think God chose Paul for a miraculous conversion, while the rest of the Israelites where left to their unfaithfulness? If you could ask Paul why God chose him, what do you think his answer would be? In these chapters, Paul's passion and love for his fellow Israelites is evident. Why does he have such passion? Do you have a

similar passion for those around you who have not yet come to Jesus?

12) At the end of the Israelites' forty year journey through the desert, Deuteronomy records three great sermons that Moses gave to the people before they proceeded into the promised land without him. Read Deuteronomy 30:11-20. Is Moses exhortation that much different that Paul's in heart and Spirit? What is different between the message of Paul and that of Moses (vv. 10:5-6)?

13) It is easy to understand why Paul tells us we need to believe in our heart (v. 10:9), but why is it important to confess with our mouth (Prov. 6:2, Mat. 12:33-37, 10:31-33, Luke 6:45)?

14) Did the Israelite nation have an opportunity to respond to the prophets (v. 10:18)? Did they have an opportunity to respond to Christ himself?

15) During Jesus' ministry, He personally and directly called people to repentance as he preached throughout Galilee and even at the temple itself. Then, on the road to Damascus (Acts 9), he called Paul directly. Since that time, the Bible records no further personal face-to-face call from Jesus out to the unfaithful. How many responded – thousands, tens of thousands (see John 6:60-71, Acts1:15)? How does Jesus intend to grow his kingdom (vv. 10:14-15, Mat. 28:16-20)?

16) In v. 10:19, Paul quotes a prophetic song that Moses spoke to the Israelites after delivering one of his final sermons. Read Deut. 32:21. According to this song, why did God choose to make Israel jealous by another nation? Paul is implying that this prophecy was being fulfilled during his time of ministry. Who is the "other nation"? What is the purpose of making the Israelites jealous?

17) In v. 10:20, Paul quotes the prophet Isaiah (Isa. 65:1-2). Through this prophecy, what does God say about the future of the Israelites (Isa. 65:8)?

18) Anyone who has been the parent of multiple children can relate to the story of Elijah that Paul relates in vv. 11:2-3. Sooner or a later, one of the children will come running to the parent, telling all the things their siblings are doing wrong and then demand that the parents "do something". What was God's response to Elijah?

Election

One of the more challenging concepts in the scriptures is the notion of election. In vv. 11:5-7 Paul explains that some people have been chosen, or elected, by God to be in a position to respond to the miraculous events of Jesus and His apostles, while others He "hardened" and thereby prevented from responding to these miracles. Further, Paul explains that God's choices are not based on our works, but then does not offer any alternative explanation about how God makes His choices. In his letters, Paul simply reminds us of God's sovereignty and, as he states in v. 11:33, *How unsearchable are his judgments and how inscrutable his ways!*

When confronted with this notion of election, many questions come to mind. Questions such as "does this mean that God loves some people more than others?" and "If God is doing the choosing, does this mean that we don't have a free will to place our faith in Jesus?"

Theologians still have not come to complete agreement on what this means and the topic is worth further study beyond the scope of this guide. Paul does give us a clue to the possible motivations of God in v. 10:19, where he quotes God's words: *I will make you jealous of those who are not a nation.* A common observation made by many who have done mission work is that they didn't appreciate the richness of the blessings they had until they saw the world of people who live without. Similarly, Allen Greenspan, former head of the U.S. Federal Reserve Board, found that people only feel wealthy if those around them have less. It seems that we are unable to appreciate blessings unless we have something to contrast them with. A global observation of the Bible is that *everything* God does, He does for *us*, so it is reasonable to assume that God's elections are done for all of us as well. When God led the Israelites out of bondage in Egypt and brought them to the promised land, He blessed every one of them. However, they quickly lost their faith. By electing to soften the hearts of a few at a time, as Paul describes, God may be maintaining sufficient contrast to allow us to grow strong in our faith – a contrast the Israelites didn't initially have. When rescuers save people from a sinking ship, they do it one boatload at a time. The don't do this because they love some passengers more than others, they simply do it this way because it works.

19) Read Mat. 13:10-17 and compare it with the scripture Paul quotes in v. 11:8. Why is it that we can understand the parables of Jesus in a way that the original hearers didn't?

20) What did the Jews of the day rely on for their salvation (vv. 2:17, 11:20)? In v. 11:9, Paul quotes David's Psalm 69. Read Psalm 69. The scriptures show us that David committed horrible crimes – he murdered entire villages of people, he stole, he committed adultery and, on his deathbed, he asked his son to murder the one man who publicly held him accountable for his wicked ways (1 Kings 2:8), and yet David was held in high regard. Jesus himself was referred to as the Son of David. What was David's attitude toward his salvation? What was he depending on?

21) In v. 11:13, Paul says that he serves the Gentiles in hopes that some of his fellow Israelites will be drawn closer to God. Do you think this was Paul's only motivation for serving the Gentiles?

22) In v. 11:18, Paul warns the Gentiles not to be arrogant. Throughout history, have their been times when the Jews were looked down on for "killing Jesus"? Have you ever felt superior because you were a Christian, or because you had more faith then someone else? What is it, in v. 11:17, that Paul says enabled us to come to the Lord? What should the attitude of our hearts be towards those that were broken off for us?

23) What warning does Paul give in vv. 11:20-23? Can you have an attitude of unkindness if you have set your mind on the things of the Spirit as Paul extolled in v. 8:5?

24) Why has a partial hardening of the heart come upon Israel? Who was the focus of Jesus' ministry (Mat. 15:24)? By what process, then, was salvation to come to the Gentiles (vv. 11:5, 10:14-15)?

25) What hope does Paul have for the Israelites?

26) It is common to wonder if God really does care for everyone since it is apparent that he has hardened some people's hearts, while softening others. What is Paul's answer to this (v. 11:32)?

27) Our written language is ideally suited for documenting rational thoughts, however, it can be a challenge to convey our emotions. Frequently, in scripture, the authors reverted to poetic language when they felt a need to share their emotions. What are the emotions that Paul is conveying in v. 11:33-36?

28) Take a look at the list of cross references in a study bible for chapters 9-11 and notice how many citations and references there are from the Old Testament scriptures. What does this say about Paul's working knowledge of the scriptures? Why did he feel the need to refer to and quote so much? At least one scholar noted that in Paul's quotation of Hosea in 9:25, he didn't use the phrase "I will say", as it was in the Septuagint (a version of the ancient scriptures available to Paul at the time), but rather "I will call". This scholar was tempted to read meaning into this "change", but as you note the fluidity of Paul's references and quotations from scripture and how he can weave them together, showing how they all support one another and support Christ, do you think it is possible that Paul was simply quoting the scriptures from memory?

ROMANS 12-15:13

Romans 12 marks a transition in Paul's letter from theology to a practical response to our relationship with God. Paul sought to convict us of our sins in the outset of his letter, then he showed us the way of salvation through our faith in Jesus. Finally, he showed us that even our faith is a merciful gift from God that was granted to us not because of anything we have earned, so that we would accept it with humility and without arrogance.

As one reads the New Testament letters, it is clear that many in the early churches did not live in this spirit of humility. The morally corrupt sexual practices of the day made their way into the church, there were still infights, arguments over theology, pride and ego issues, and complaints about the politics of the day. Paul was aware of all this and realized that these were symptoms of people who were not living in the spirit of our living God, the God for whom John succinctly stated: "is love" (1 John 4:8).

These remaining chapters of Romans are particularly relevant to us because not a single problem of the early church does not still exist today. In fact, we can add to them fights over the color of the carpet, the style of worship, and any number of other things that cause discord within our churches. Worse still, many have become quite adept at picking and choosing verses of the Bible to use as weapons against one another during these squabbles.

It should be enough for us learn to *set the mind on the Spirit* (v. 8.6), but we stubbornly hold onto those evil desires of the flesh and so Paul spends his next few chapters breaking down for us what it means to have a spirit of love. It would be almost comical that he has to lay this out for us in such clarity if we didn't need to hear it so desperately.

As you begin your study of these last few chapters of Romans, take special care to read his words not only with your head, but also with your heart.

1) In what ways can you present your bodies as a living sacrifice (v. 12:1)?

2) In v. 12:2, Paul presents some of the most profound and useful advice of the Bible: *Do not be conformed to this world, but be transformed by the renewal of your mind.* How does this advice relate to the concept of *dikaiosune* (righteousness) discussed in Rom. 3? Some say that it is our actions that count, but what did Jesus say about adultery (Mat. 5:28)? When we seek to be more like Christ, which is more useful, learning to control our actions, or learning to control our thoughts?

3) How often to you pray loving and compassionate prayers for your family? Your neighbors and co-workers? The various strangers that come into our lives each day? How often do you ask yourself: "How can I express Christ's love to them today?" Does this type of prayer time with Jesus contribute to your sanctification?

4) In v. 12:3, Paul indicates, more clearly, that it is God that has assigned us faith in different measures. How did Jesus grow his faith (v. 4:20)? How do we get our faith (v. 10:17, 2 Cor. 10:14-15)? How do we grow our faith (Luke 19:11-27 – *The parable of the Ten Minas*, James 1:2-3, Mal. 3:9-10, Jude 1:20)?

5) It is common, within the church (and also within the workplace), to criticize others who do not have our skills and talents. In vv. 12:4-8 Paul reminds us that we have each been gifted with different skills and talents. We forget that God loves each of his unique children more than a young mother loves her toddlers. If someone started to point out the faults and shortcomings of a child in front of their mother, how would that mother feel? When you think critical things of others, and mentally focus on their shortcomings, how do you think the Lord feels? Aren't you always before Him so that he

can hear your thoughts and words?

6) In the vv. 12:4-8 Paul was making two points, the first is that we need to learn to appreciate and depend on each other, what is the other major point?

7) In vv. 12:9-21 Paul provides guidance on how we should live within society. (In reference to v. 12:20, Paul is quoting Proverbs 25 which makes reference to an ancient Egyptian ritual where a person would carry a pan of burning coals on his head as a sign of his repentance.) Which of these do you struggle with the most? Why?

8) In vv. 13:1-7, Paul shares with us how a Christian should view their government. At the time of this writing, the church was

living under the sometimes harsh Roman authority. These words can be a challenge to understand. Should the citizens living under oppressive regimes (think Hitler or Mussolini) stand back and let persecutions continue? Jesus himself lived under such a repressive regime and yet he never mentioned a word about overthrowing the Romans, much to the disappointment of Judas. Why did Jesus not concern himself with this? What were His priorities?

9) In vv. 13:8-10, Paul encourages people to follow the commandments. Is he encouraging people to go back to depending on the Law? What is he really saying? In v. 13:14, Paul tells us to *put on the Lord Jesus Christ, and make no provision for the flesh, to gratify its desires.* In what ways do we make provisions for the flesh? What does he mean by *put on the Lord Jesus Christ?*

10) On the Internet you can find large charts that map out the various denominations of the Christian church. Over the course of Paul's ministry, when the faith was very young, he was confronted with new believers that had quite varying views of how to honor their faith. In vv. 14:1-9 Paul shares the wisdom he has gathered in dealing with these variations. How do you think Paul would feel to find that whole charts were necessary

to map out the divisions of the Church?

11) In v. 14:14, Paul states: *I know and am persuaded in the Lord Jesus that nothing is unclean in itself, but it is unclean for anyone who thinks it unclean* and in vv. 14:22-23 he says: *The faith that you have, keep between yourself and God. Blessed is the one who has no reason to pass judgment on himself for what he approves. But whoever has doubts is condemned if he eats, because the eating is not from faith. For whatever does not proceed from faith is sin.* Does this mean that each of us gets to invent our own morality? What does Paul really mean by this?

12) Siblings will sometimes fight viciously with each other for the right to carry a gift to one of their parents. The parents may appreciate that this child brought them a gift, but how much more appreciative would they be if their children shared love for one another? As Christians, we sometimes seek to honor God at the expense of one another. For example, when you dress for Church, do you ask yourself: *In what way could my dress be a stumbling block for others?* Would a person of little means feel like they belong in a church where everyone else is in expensive dress clothes? We can also seek to honor or highlight ourselves at the expense of others. Would other members of the church feel distracted if you wore provocative clothing or a T-shirt with

lewd sayings? Have you ever judged someone by how they chose to dress? In vv. 14:13-23 Paul gives guidance on these things. Should we seek, and expect others to seek, God's approval through the clothes we wear or the music we play, or do we rather give God pleasure by how we serve Christ? In this passage, how is Paul suggesting we serve Christ?

13) Earlier in Paul's letter, we learned that God justifies us through our faith, but then as we work as "slaves of righteousness", we grow in our sanctification (v. 6:20). Should we extend the same courtesy to those of weaker faith, that Jesus is showing to us (vv. 15:1-13)? Should we accept others as they are, with all their weakness, with all their tendencies to fall back to their earthly desires, so that we can keep ourselves in a position to gently, and lovingly encourage them in the Lord so that their faith will grow? How easy is it for us to carelessly work against the Lord (vv. 14:20-21)?

14) In v. 14:5, Paul describes God as the God of endurance and encouragement. Do you find that you extend the same patient endurance to others that God has extended to you? If not, why is this? Have you trained yourself to be a spring of encouragement to all those around you? Do you think that

those around you have no need of encouragement? If so, why have you failed to get to know them well? In v. 15:8, Paul tells us Jesus came to show God's truthfulness. By what means did Jesus say He did this (Mat. 15:24)? Is it worth imitating Christ in this (in servanthood)? How well are you doing this?

15) Paul's letter was intended to bring about much self reflection on the part of the hearers and Paul knows that they, as he himself felt at times, may not have faired well in their own self-evaluations. However, do you believe that God wishes His believers to be downcast, depressed, or wallowing in guilt? What is it that God provides for us as an antidote for these feelings? What emotions does God want us to experience (see v. 15:13)? Is this what you experience? If not, then re-read chapter 15 and notice the relational aspects of his words. How can we build each other up for each other's good if we have not established intimate personal relationships with fellow Christians? Would your feelings of joy and peace be enhanced with close Christians friends with whom you mutually encourage and edify each other?

16) If Paul's exhortations and encouraged self-reflection were not meant to depress us, what were they for?

ROMANS 15:14-16

In the opening of Paul's letter to the Romans, he thanked God *because your faith is proclaimed in all the world.* He then proceeded to tear them down and rebuild them on a firm theological foundation and then encouraged them to change their ways and live according to the Spirit. Paul begins the close of his letter by closing this criticism sandwich with the words: *I myself am satisfied about you, my brothers, that you yourselves are full of goodness, filled with all knowledge and able to instruct one another.*

This final portion of the letter also gives us more personal insight into the heart and motivation of Paul and serves to give us a glimpse of the close personal relationships that he himself built in the years he spent spreading the gospel of Christ.

1) Paul mentions, in v. 15:15, that he wrote boldly on *some* points to remind them. Can you think of an important area of the Christian walk which Paul failed to mention? Paul could have simply ignored these Christian churches that he had heard about. There was a great risk that writing such a critical letter to some other church would result in harsh personal rejection, and it would be easy for both Paul and the church to believe that their spiritual welfare and habits were none of his business. Why did Paul write anyway? Is it important for Christians to hold each other accountable? Is there value in allowing others to hold us accountable? What lessons can we learn from Paul's

letter that teaches *how* to hold each other accountable?

2) What was Paul's view of his own missionary calling (vv. 15:15-21)? Did the Holy Spirit confirm this view (v. 15:22)?

3) What enabled the success of Paul's missionary work (vv. 15:18-19)?

4) In vv. 15:24-29 Paul makes a subtle appeal for money. What two distinct Godly purposes require financial support? Do these needs still exist today? Do you resent pastors or priests when they ask for money? Why? How do you choose how much to give? What does the Bible tell us (2 Cor. 9:6-8, 8:1-15)?

5) In vv. 15:30-33 Paul asks for prayer that he *be delivered from the unbelievers in Judea.* How did his return trip go (Acts 21:27-28)? When people ask you for prayers, do you take the request seriously? Are you afraid to ask others for prayer when you face challenging circumstances? If not, then do you think God intends us to walk in faith alone? What can you do to gather friends or increase the depth of your relationships so that you can feel comfortable asking for prayer?

6) It was customary in the early church for a Christian to bring with themselves a *Letter of Commendation* from their home church when moving or traveling so that the new church would welcome them (see vv. Col 4:7-11). In vv. 16:1-2, we see Paul give such a commendation to Phoebe, who apparently carried this letter (either alone or, more likely, with a group) to the churches in Rome. What does v. 16:2 say about Paul's relationship with Phoebe?

Combining a textual analysis of the scriptures, archeological evidence, and an understanding of naming traditions at the time, it is possible to derive a speculative, but plausible understanding of the people whom Paul wished greeted. Such an understanding (listed below) can provide additional insight into Paul's motivations for his greetings.

Priscilla and Aquila – Married, Jewish (see Acts 18, 1 Cor. 16:19) and tentmakers by trade. Hosted a church in their home on Aventine Hill, an area of town with higher social status.

Epaenetus – Jewish (1 Cor. 16:15), a servant in the household of Stephanas.

Mary – Jewish, a feed slave and Roman citizen.

Andronicus and Junia – Married, likely related to Paul, their names are Greek in origin.

Ampliatus – Jewish, either a current, or freed slave.

Urbanus – A Roman official.

Stachys – A gentile.

Apelles – Jewish.

The household of Aristobulus – Refers to the slaves of this house. Apparently Aristobulus himself was not a believer.

Herodion – Apparently related to Paul and therefore Jewish, possibly a freed slave from the household of Aristobulus.

The family of Narcissus – Refers to the slaves of this house. Narcissus was executed by Nero as a traitor in AD 54, at which point the slaves became property of Nero.

Tryphena and Tryphosa – Sisters, and freed slaves.

Persis – The name Persis means "Persian woman". Likely a slave or freed slave.

Rufus – Jewish and likely the son of Simon of Cyrene who carried the cross of Jesus (see Mark 15:21).

Asyncritus – Slave, and immigrant to Rome, of low social status.

Phlegon – Slave or freedman and immigrant to Rome, of low social status.

Hermas – Gentile and immigrant to Rome, of low social status.

Patrobus – Prominent freedman, possibly in the imperial administration, immigrant to Rome, of low social status.

Hermes – Slave, immigrant to Rome, of low social status.

Asyncritus, Phlegon, Hermas, Patrobus, and Hermes appear to

be leaders of a church in the tenements of Trastevere or Porta Capena.

Philologus and Julia – Married, slaves, possibly immigrants to Rome.
Nereus – Slave.
Olympas – Slave and immigrant.

Philologus and Julia, Nereus, and Olympas, appear to be leaders of another church located in the tenements of Rome.

7) Since Prisca and Aquila had been hosting a church in their home, why do you think Paul felt a need to share some of their story with the church? Wouldn't the rest of the church already know about them (see vv. 14:1-3)? Note that in chapter 16, Paul similarly edifies several others who are already in Rome.

8) In vv. 16:3-15, the word *Aspazomai* , translated as *greet*, is more than just a "hello". *Aspazomai* has a connotation of grabbing someone in a big and joyfull bear hug. Note that Paul isn't telling the church to "say hello for me", he is telling them to say hello to each other (v. 16:16). Why does Paul feel the need to say this and what is he trying to accomplish with these admonitions? (Refer also to the section on church history in the introductory section of this study guide.)

9) How do you think these individuals felt as they first heard themselves being edified, by name, as Paul's letter was being read aloud in church? How would this have affected their spirit and motivation to continue serving Christ? How often do you edify your fellow brothers and sisters in Christ to others?

10) Although the names referenced in vv. 16:1-15 appear to include those who have not been universally welcomed, or treated respectfully, in the broader church in Rome, what can you discern about the cultural, gender, and social make-up of the early Christian church?

11) What, does it seem, is Paul's greatest fear for the Church (vv. 16:17-18)?

12) Within 20 miles (30 km) of your home, are there other churches with members of different social or cultural backgrounds than that of your own church? Do you believe that these churches work together in the unity and spirit in which Paul was trying to promote to the disparate churches in Rome?

13) In modern society, Paul has been chastised for "putting women down" in his writings (see vv. 1 Tim 2:11-12). In Romans 16, however, we get a different perspective. From this chapter, how do you think Paul views the efforts of women in the church?

14) Why does Paul specifically mention Erastus' job title (v. 16:23)?

15) How does Paul's final prayer support the justification for his

theology (vv. 16:25-27)?

16) Undoubtedly, during the course of this study, the questions and discussions have led you to realize that there are opportunities for growth in various areas of your walk. Which areas, for you personally, do you need to grow in? Write down a list of these areas and, for each of them, make a note of how you would like to grow in that area. (The act of writing this down and then sharing what your wrote in a discussion group will help clarify your thoughts.) Do you have a close friend or group of friends that can help keep you accountable and guide your heart on these things?

30603378R00051

Made in the USA
Lexington, KY
09 March 2014